DON'T
KNOW
MUCH
ABOUT®

THE

KINGS &
QUEENS

OF ENGLAND

KENNETH C. DAVIS

ILLUSTRATED BY S. D. SCHINDLER

HarperCollinsPublishers

Acknowledgments

An author's name goes on the cover of a book. But behind that book are a great many people who make it all happen. I would like to thank all of the wonderful people at HarperCollins who helped make this book a reality, including Susan Katz, Kate Morgan Jackson, Barbara Lalicki, Harriett Barton, Rosemary Brosnan, Anne Dunn, Dana Hayward, Maggie Herold, Fumi Kosaka, Rachel Orr, and Katherine Rogers. I would also like to thank David Black, Joy Tutela, and Alix Reid for their friendship, assistance, and great ideas. My wife, Joann, and my children, Jenny and Colin, are always a source of inspiration, joy, and support. Without them, I could not do my work.

I especially thank April Prince for her devoted efforts and unique contributions. This book would not have been possible without her tireless work, imagination, and creativity.

This is a Don't Know Much About® book.
Don't Know Much About® is the trademark of Kenneth C. Davis.

Don't Know Much About® the Kings and Queens of England
Copyright © 2002 by Kenneth C. Davis
Printed in the U.S.A. All rights reserved.
www.harperchildrens.com

Library of Congress Cataloging-in-Publication Data
Davis, Kenneth C.
Don't know much about the kings and queens of England / by Kenneth C. Davis ; illustrated by S. D. Schindler.
    p.   cm.—(Don't know much)
  ISBN 0-06-028611-3 — ISBN 0-06-028612-1 (lib. bdg.)
1. Great Britain—Kings and rulers—Biography—Juvenile literature.
2. Queens—Great Britain—Biography—Juvenile literature.   [1. Kings, queens, rulers, etc.—Miscellanea.   2. Great Britain—History—Miscellanea.   3. Questions and answers.]   I. Schindler, S. D., ill.   II. Title.   III. Series.
DA28.1 .D39   2002   00-038898
941'.009'9—dc21
[B]

Design by Charles Yuen
1 2 3 4 5 6 7 8 9 10
❖
First Edition

"This blessed plot, this earth, this realm, this England

This nurse, this teeming womb of royal kings, . . .

This land of such dear souls, this dear dear land."

—William Shakespeare, *Richard II,* act 2, scene 1

We all know about King Arthur and the knights of the Round Table. We know about the king who was in his counting house, counting out his money, while his queen was eating bread and honey. And you've surely heard about that Queen of Hearts who ate some tarts. (Queens do more than eat, I am certain!) They are the kings and queens of nursery rhymes and legends.

But *Don't Know Much About® the Kings and Queens of England* tells the story of the *real* kings and queens of England, people whose stories are much more interesting and surprising than the stories about made-up kings and queens. There have been good and bad kings and queens. Some did great things. Some could be very cruel. Just ask two of the six wives of Henry VIII. Oops! They can't answer. They've lost their heads!

Like other Don't Know Much About® books, this one proves that real history about real people is a lot more fun than a bunch of simple dates and facts. And the true stories of some of the most famous monarchs of England are much more fascinating than you'd ever imagine.

This book highlights some of the most interesting kings and queens of England but does not discuss them all. For a complete chronological list of all the kings and queens of England, please see page 48.

Dates shown in headings next to the names of kings and queens indicate how long the monarch reigned.

GUESS WHICH OF THESE WERE DUTIES OF THE KING. TO:

A. keep law and order and punish criminals

B. represent God, who it was believed had chosen the king as ruler

C. own land

D. spend his people's money

E. lead the royal army in battle

F. all of the above

The answer is *F*. The king was a busy man! Does a king or queen of England have these same duties today? When you get to the end of the book, you'll know the answer!

WHO WAS WILLIAM, AND WHY WAS HE CALLED THE CONQUEROR?

William the Conqueror was ruler of the part of northern France called Normandy. William also happened to be the cousin of King Edward III (Edward the Confessor) of England. Since King Edward didn't have any sons, he may have promised William the throne after he died. But when Edward died, Harold Godwinson, the richest nobleman in England, took over the throne instead. This made William very, very angry—so angry that he came and *conquered*, or took over, England from King Harold.

WHY DID WILLIAM'S ARMY RUN AND HIDE DURING THE BATTLE OF HASTINGS?

William's men were pretending they'd given up. When Harold's men followed, William's army turned around and led a surprise attack. King Harold was killed, and William of Normandy, who didn't speak a word of English, became king of England.

Living in a castle wasn't much fun in William's day. Castles were built to protect their owners, not to make them comfortable. They were cold, stony, drafty places to live.

How were battles fought in William's day?

William lived before there were guns and cannons. Armies fought with swords and even sometimes with their fists. Most of William's men fought on horseback. Many fought with bow and arrows, and a few used long spears. They wore cone-shaped helmets with noseguards and long shirts of chain mail, or armor made of thousands of tiny iron rings linked together. They held long, kite-shaped shields. King Harold's men fought a little differently. They couldn't afford horses, so they held their two-handled battle-axes and stood close together to make a wall of shields. The only way William could get his arrows past the shield wall was to get Harold's men to break apart and come running after him, so that's what he did.

What palace towers over London, England's capital city?

William built castles all over England, but the biggest and most impressive castle of all was the Tower of London. The Tower was the king's home. It was also a prison where people who committed crimes against the king were tortured and killed. Over the years, various kings and queens added on a royal mint (where coins are made), a royal zoo, and a safe place to keep the crown jewels.

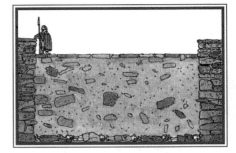

Some of the Tower of London's walls are so thick that, if they were hollow, you and four or five friends could lie down end to end inside them!

To celebrate the victory at Hastings, William's half-brother, the Bishop of Bayeux, ordered a magnificent piece of needlework. The 230-foot-long Bayeux Tapestry is an amazing record of the Battle of Hastings and all the events leading up to it.

HENRY II (1154-1189)

It's said that, around the time of Henry II, a man named Robin Hood lived with his merry men in Sherwood Forest. Robin Hood robbed from the rich and gave to the poor. Why? Because the king's sheriffs took too much money from the poor and kept it for themselves. Was Robin Hood a real man? No one knows for sure.

WHO WAS THE FIRST ROYAL BOOKWORM?

King Henry II always had either a book or a bow in his hands. Henry loved to read and was the first English *monarch*, or ruler of a country, to read before going to bed. Quite a change from William the Conqueror, who couldn't read or even sign his own name!

TRUE OR FALSE: ENGLAND'S KING HENRY II RULED OVER MORE OF FRANCE THAN THE KING OF FRANCE.

True. Even though he was King of England, Henry had land in northern France from his parents, and in southern France from his French wife, Eleanor of Aquitaine.

WAS ELEANOR OF AQUITAINE DIFFERENT FROM OTHER WOMEN OF HER TIME?

Yes. Eleanor had more land than any other woman in Europe. This made her rich and powerful. She made business deals and even ruled when Henry was away. These things might not sound unusual to you today, but in Eleanor's day, a queen's job was to have children.

HENRY III (1216-1272)

WHERE IN LONDON MIGHT YOU HAVE MET A POLAR BEAR OR CAMEL?

At the Tower of London! King Henry III was the best zookeeper in Europe. In his zoo at the Tower, he kept a camel, a polar bear from the king of Norway, three leopards from the emperor of Prussia, a lion from the king of France, and the only elephant Englishmen had ever seen.

COULD KING HENRY III MAKE ANY LAW HE WANTED TO?

Not at all. And he had his dear old dad, the unpopular King John, to blame for it. King John was so greedy that the *nobles,* or rich families who had lots of land and power, made him sign a document called the *Magna Carta,* or Great Charter. The Magna Carta said the king couldn't arrest people just because he felt like it or force taxes on anyone he pleased. King John signed the Magna Carta in 1215, but that didn't mean he or his son always obeyed what it said. In fact, in 1265, a nobleman named Simon de Montfort invited other nobles to form a council that would put the king in his place once and for all. This group of Englishmen was essentially the first *Parliament*. Today England's Parliament is like our Congress, the group of officials we choose to help our president make laws.

Seven hundred years' worth of royal bones are in London's Westminster Abbey, where most English kings and queens were crowned, married, and buried. (A minster is a big or important church.) The church was first built in 1052, but King Henry III rebuilt it to make it even more grand.

HOW DID KING EDWARD I GET HIS NICKNAME, LONGSHANKS?

Hint: Your "shank" is the part of your leg from your knee to your ankle.

So Edward got his name from being especially long-legged and tall. Today it's not unusual for men to be six feet tall, like King Edward was, but back then people didn't grow as tall.

WAS EDWARD A "LUCKY DUCK"?

King Edward really loved his wife, Eleanor. This was rare because royal marriages were usually about business partnerships between countries, not about love.

King Edward I was a great soldier who had unbelievable luck.

• Lightning passed over the king's shoulder and killed two people behind him.

• In the middle of a game of chess, Edward got up and left. Seconds later, a huge stone from the castle wall fell and landed right where the king had been sitting.

EDWARD III (1327-1377)

WHO WAS KING EDWARD III'S STORYBOOK HERO?

Hint: The hero lived in a castle in Camelot with his wife, Guinevere, and had Merlin the Wizard for his teacher.

King Edward III loved the stories of—you guessed it—King Arthur. King Edward lived during the Middle Ages, a time when there were fancy tournaments for knights in shining armor. Like King Arthur, King Edward believed in the knightly values of honor, courage, fairness, protection of women, and loyalty to the king.

WHAT WEIGHED HEAVILY ON A KNIGHT?

A knight's armor could weigh one hundred pounds. (Some knights were so heavy they had to be hoisted onto their horses with poles, pulleys, and ropes!) If a knight fell from his horse, he could only lie there helplessly like a beetle on its back.

King Arthur: Fact or fiction?

There was never a king of England named Arthur, so who was this guy? The legend of King Arthur was probably inspired by a real English warrior who lived about 1,500 years ago. Whether his name was Arthur, we'll never know. But we do know that the knightly stories of King Arthur must be made up—because there were no knights or castles until about 500 years after he was supposed to have lived!

13

WHAT WAS A KNIGHT'S DAY LIKE?

To be a knight in King Edward III's day, you had to have years of training in military skill and manners and lots of money to pay for your armor. Here's what your life would be like:

Today knighthood isn't a job as a soldier but an honor for doing something good for England. All kinds of people, from scientists to schoolteachers, actors, and even U.S. presidents, are knights. The queen approves about thirty-five hundred knights each year. Knights are called Sir, their wives Lady. Women who receive the honor are called Dame.

At age seven, you would go to live at a knight's house and become a *page*. (Today's word *pager* comes from this word.) You'd clean armor and practice archery, sword fighting, singing, and dancing. You'd learn good manners, especially toward ladies, and you'd serve the knights and ladies at the table, like a waiter.

At age fourteen or fifteen, you'd become a *squire,* or a knight's attendant. You would help the knight get dressed (which could take an hour!) and accompany him to tournaments—and maybe even into battle.

When you were twenty-one, you would finally be made a knight yourself. Though the ceremony was often performed by the king, any knight could tap you on the shoulder with his sword and pronounce you a knight.

WHAT WAS THE BLACK DEATH?

The Black Death was the nickname for a terrible disease called bubonic plague. The plague hit London in 1348 and may have killed as many as one out of every three people in England in just ten years. Whole families and even entire villages were wiped out. Doctors suggested some crazy cures— like swallowing the powder of crushed emeralds or shaving a live chicken's bottom and strapping it to a plague sore! Nothing worked. Centuries later, doctors learned that the infection was caused by bacteria that lived in fleas. The fleas got it from infected rats and passed it on to humans through their bite.

DID KING RICHARD II STARVE THE POOR?

Not directly. But King Richard demanded so much money from them that many poor people didn't have enough left to buy food. So a man named Wat Tyler led a Peasants' Revolt to London, where the hungry farmers burned buildings and killed two of the king's men. This made King Richard say he would end *serfdom*, a kind of slavery. The king didn't keep his promise, but serfdom died out soon by itself.

WHAT DID KING RICHARD OWN THAT NO ENGLISH KING OWNED BEFORE HIM?

A handkerchief! This was a sign of the king's good manners. Richard held royal banquets and surrounded himself with paintings, poetry, high fashion, and minstrels who sang and played music. The royal *court,* or the palace and advisors, servants, family, and friends that surround the monarch, became a place where the king could display his good taste, money, and power. Before that, the court had been used mostly to plan wars and battles.

Since there was no standard English, people spelled words however they wanted. Just think— no spelling tests at school!

୨୨୨୨୨୨୨୨୨

Did Richard II and his people speak the same English we do today?

See for yourself!
People in
King Richard's

day said:	We say:
daed	*day*
monath	*month*
modor	*mother*
gan	*go*
drincan	*drink*

HENRY V (1413-1422)

WHAT COUNTRY DID KING HENRY V TAKE OVER?

Hint: It was William the Conqueror's home, and, scrambled, its letters are ENRCFA.

Henry took over France. The French and English had been fighting for more than seventy-five years when Henry V became king. The determined Henry won one of the greatest victories in English history at the Battle of Agincourt in 1415. Even though the French had many more soldiers, the English had better weapons. Their powerful longbows, which were as tall as the soldiers themselves, were faster to load and more accurate than the smaller French crossbows.

HOW LONG DID THE HUNDRED YEARS' WAR LAST?

The English and French fought the Hundred Years' War for 116 years, from 1337 to 1453. (Hey, when you're at war that long, who's counting?) The countries fought, on and off and back and forth, because they couldn't decide who should rule what. That's because, thanks to our conquering pal, William, the royal families of both countries shared some royal blood. They also shared the same language—Henry V's father, King Henry IV, was the first king of England to speak English instead of French as his native language.

English had been England's official language since 1362, but many people, including the king and his court, still spoke the French of William the Conqueror. Books were written in French or Latin until a poet named Geoffrey Chaucer wrote a great story called *The Canterbury Tales* in English.

King Henry won so much land in France that he was supposed to become king of France when the French king died. But Henry didn't live that long.

SO WHO FINALLY WON THE HUNDRED YEARS' WAR?

Well, no one, really. The war ended when the French won their land back from King Henry VI. And things were about the same as they'd been before the whole war started.

WHAT HAPPENED TO THE PRINCES IN THE TOWER?

The Hundred Years' War was over, but still there was a battle for the throne. King Henry VI lost his crown to King Edward IV, then gained it back, then lost it again. When King Edward IV died, his twelve-year-old son, King Edward V, should have taken the throne. But before there was even time to crown the new king, he and his younger brother mysteriously disappeared in the Tower of London. Many people think that Richard III, Edward IV's younger brother, murdered the princes so he could be king. There's no proof of this, but in 1674 skeletons of two young boys were found in a chest buried ten feet under a flight of stairs in the Tower. If only the bones could talk . . .

Joan of Arc was a teenage peasant girl who became a hero to the French. During the Hundred Years' War, Joan started hearing voices. She said the voices were Catholic saints telling her to lead the French soldiers against the English. Young Joan cut her hair and dressed in full armor to lead the French to victory. Later she was captured by the English and found guilty of witchcraft and heresy, or going against the values of the church. For this, she was burned to death. Almost five hundred years later, she was made a saint.

WHAT THORNY SITUATION DID KING HENRY VII GET HIS COUNTRY OUT OF?

The English had stopped fighting the French just in time to start fighting themselves in the Wars of the Roses. But these wars weren't fought over any flowers. They got their name from the symbols of the two families who were fighting for the crown: the House of York (the white rose) and the House of Lancaster (the red rose). The wars were fought off and on from 1455 to 1485 until Richard III (of York) was killed at the Battle of

Bosworth in 1485. His crown went to Henry VII (of Lancaster). By this time, most of England's money had been spent on war. King Henry worked hard to make money and keep peace.

WHERE WAS KING HENRY'S "NEWFOUND LAND"?

During Henry's reign, European traders started sailing to Asia to buy tea and spices. In 1496 Henry paid an explorer named John Cabot to find a shorter, quicker route to the East by sailing west. Cabot returned and mistakenly said he'd landed in Asia. He didn't know he'd really landed in North America. (Today Newfoundland is part of Canada.) When the place Cabot landed was found to be a whole new world a few years later, the land in the Americas didn't seem important. But that would change in about one hundred years, when people like the Pilgrims wanted to go to that part of the world.

Was Henry's wife, Elizabeth of York, the Queen of Hearts?

She was, and she still is. She's the queen you see every time you play cards. She must have been really good at winning Henry's heart, since Henry was a Lancaster and she was an enemy York. The marriage finally forced the two families to get along.

HENRY VIII (1509-1547)

A not-so-foolish thing about life at court was having to move from palace to palace every few months. The court had to move so that the palace they'd just lived in could be "aired and cleaned." There were no indoor toilets and people hardly ever bathed, so it's no wonder the palaces started to smell!

WHY COULD KING HENRY VIII BE CALLED BIG RED?

Big Red wasn't King Henry's nickname, but it could have been. Henry was a dashing redhead whose big body matched his big personality. No English king or queen in history has been as powerful or famous as King Henry VIII.

WHAT WAS KING HENRY VIII REALLY GOOD AT?

Spending money! Henry liked to show how rich and powerful he was by entertaining guests at fancy banquets and building lots of ships for his navy. (In fact, he built the largest ship anyone had ever seen and named it the *Great Harry*—Harry being his own nickname!) He also showed his power by declaring himself king of Ireland.

DID KING HENRY VIII WRITE A SONG OR A BOOK?

Both. King Henry was not only very powerful, he was also very talented. He could dance and play the harp and organ, and many people say he wrote a song called "Greensleeves." Henry VIII was also the first king of England to be the author of a printed book.

WHAT WAS THE MOST FOOLISH PART ABOUT HENRY'S COURT?

His fools! Henry VIII not only liked to entertain other people at his parties, he liked to *be* entertained. This was done by his *fools,* or members of the court whose jobs were to make the king laugh. Fools wore funny bright clothes and shoes with curled toes. They were sometimes bald or dyed their hair to match their clothes. When ordered, a fool told jokes and stories or did somersaults and tricks.

WHAT IS KING HENRY VIII FAMOUS FOR HAVING SIX OF?

Palaces? Crowns? No. Henry VIII had six *wives*. Who were the wives, and what became of them?

I   Henry wanted to divorce his first wife, Catherine of Aragon, because she hadn't given birth to a male heir. But the leaders of the Catholic Church wouldn't allow it, so Henry just started his own church, put himself in charge, and granted *himself* a divorce.

II   Henry married his second wife, Anne Boleyn, in a secret wedding, because he wasn't divorced from Catherine of Aragon yet. When Anne gave birth to a girl instead of a boy and then had three failed pregnancies, Henry accused Anne of being unfaithful and had her beheaded at the Tower.

III   The good news: Henry's third wife, Jane Seymour, finally gave the king what he'd been waiting for—a son. The bad news: Jane died from giving birth to Prince Edward.

IV   Henry's advisors set up his fourth marriage, to the German Anne of Cleves, as a business arrangement. But when Henry saw Anne for the first time, he thought she was so ugly that he ended the marriage.

V   Everything was fine with Henry's fifth wife, Catherine Howard, until the king learned that his queen was in love with one of his advisors. Henry had her head cut off.

VI   Henry married his sixth wife, Catherine Parr, because he was sickly and lonely. As he got older, his waist had grown to fifty-four inches—you wouldn't have been able to fit your arms around him! Catherine took good care of Henry until he died at age fifty-five.

To remember what happened to each of Henry's wives, just remember this rhyme: Divorced, beheaded, died; divorced, beheaded, survived.

21

Around this time, torture devices were used to force people to confess to crimes. Some of the worst were the *brakes*, which forced your teeth out, and the *rack*, which stretched your body until your joints tore apart.

DID KING HENRY VIII START A NEW RELIGION?

Nope. Henry's Church of England was pretty much the same as the Catholic Church, except Henry was in charge. But a new religion *was* started around this time by people who were protesting the ways of the Catholic Church. These *Protestants* thought many of the Catholic officials were dishonest, and they didn't believe in the authority of the pope.

King Henry VIII's son, King Edward VI, was a strong Protestant. He decided to make Henry's Church of England Protestant, and that's the way it is today.

Prisoners entering the Tower of London were brought to their cells by boat. There was a scary-looking iron gate over the River Thames, which flowed right into the Tower grounds. The entrance became known as Traitor's Gate.

MARY I (1553-1558)

WHO WAS ENGLAND'S FIRST PROPERLY CROWNED QUEEN?

King Henry VIII's oldest daughter became Queen Mary, the first woman to inherit the crown. (All the queens you've read about so far were queens because they married a king of England.) There was one queen before Mary, the Lady Jane Grey, but Jane was never crowned. She had come to the throne because Mary's brother, King Edward VI, had wanted a Protestant to rule after him. So instead of naming his Catholic half sister Mary as his successor, he chose a distant Protestant relative, Lady Jane Grey. Jane ruled for only nine days—the shortest reign in English history—before Mary came and took the throne.

Queen Mary and her half sister, Elizabeth, had never been friends. So when a group of men was caught planning to kill Mary and put Elizabeth on the throne instead, the Queen was sure Elizabeth was involved. Mary threw her sister in jail in the Tower of London. But finally she had to let her go because she couldn't prove Elizabeth guilty. Mary sent her sister to live in a faraway, run-down palace.

WHY WEREN'T ANY QUEENS BEFORE MARY IN CHARGE OF RULING ENGLAND?

Most people thought that women shouldn't rule because they were too weak. Boy, were they wrong about Mary! Queen Mary thought all her *subjects,* or people she ruled over, should be Catholic. She ordered Protestants who wouldn't become Catholics burned at the stake. Almost three hundred people died this slow and painful death during Bloody Mary's reign.

TRUE OR FALSE: QUEEN ELIZABETH I GAVE HER COUNTRY A MAKEOVER.

True! After Queen Mary's bloody reign, England's people were thrilled to have Queen Elizabeth on the throne. Though Elizabeth declared the country Protestant, she let her subjects worship as they chose. People enjoyed plays, poetry, and fashion, and a powerful navy brought wonderful treasures from around the world. "Good Queen Bess" created "Merrie England," the strongest and richest nation in the world.

If Queen Elizabeth had married, her husband would have been a prince, not a king, even though when a king gets married, his wife becomes queen. That's still true today.

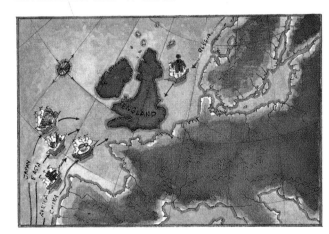

WHERE DID CHINA DISHES COME FROM DURING ELIZABETH'S REIGN?

From the country of China. (Imagine that!) Trading with faraway countries became a big deal in Elizabeth's day. Can you match the item with the place it came from?

spices	Russia
silk	China
pottery plates	Japan
carved wood	East Asia
furs	Africa

spices—East Asia, silk—Japan, pottery plates—China, carved wood—Africa, furs—Russia

WHO WAS THE STATE OF VIRGINIA, IN THE UNITED STATES, NAMED AFTER?

It was named for the Virgin Queen, Elizabeth's nickname because she never married. The present-day state of Virginia and lots of land around it were named by Sir Walter Raleigh, the first Englishman to start a colony in America.

Raleigh's settlement was started at Roanoke Island (which is now part of North Carolina) in 1587. It became known as the Lost Colony because within three years, all the settlers and their homes had mysteriously disappeared.

WHO DID QUEEN ELIZABETH LOVE MOST OF ALL?

Her people. In fact, the queen loved her subjects so much that her answer to all the men who wanted to marry her was "I am already bound to a husband. I have already joined myself in marriage to a husband, namely, the Kingdom of England." Parliament wanted Elizabeth to marry so she would have a Protestant heir to the throne. But the queen didn't want to be distracted from her job. Next in line for the throne was Elizabeth's Catholic cousin, Mary Queen of Scots. When Mary was found helping in a plan to kill Queen Elizabeth, the queen had her cousin beheaded.

Legend has it that one of Queen Elizabeth's suitors, Sir Walter Raleigh, once laid his coat over a puddle so the Queen wouldn't have to step in it.

92·92·92·92·92·92·92

An *armada* is a group of warships. The Spanish Armada was the biggest and most famous in the world—until the English changed that. Using some ships built by Elizabeth's father, King Henry VIII, and many more owned by the English people, the English destroyed the Spanish ships when they attacked in 1588. Now England ruled the seas!

WHAT FAMOUS AUTHOR'S WORDS ARE YOU USING IF YOU SAY YOU'RE: TONGUE-TIED, DEAD AS A DOORNAIL, GOING ON A WILD GOOSE CHASE, OR VANISHED INTO THIN AIR?

You're quoting William Shakespeare, probably the most famous playwright who ever lived. Shakespeare was also an actor and poet who invented two thousand English words and expressions—like *eyeball*, *alligator*, *puppy dog*, *excellent*, *silliness*, and *puke*!

WHO WAS ONE OF SHAKESPEARE'S BIGGEST FANS?

Queen Elizabeth herself. Many of Shakespeare's plays were performed for the first time at her court. There were other bursts of creativity and learning in Elizabeth's day, too. This time was called the *Renaissance*, which means "rebirth." The queen herself spoke six languages, wrote music and poetry, and was a wonderful dancer.

You could be an actor in Elizabethan England if: You were a man, a good singer and dancer, able to fight with a real sword and perform stunts, and not afraid to get wet. Most plays in Elizabethan England had lots of action and adventure. Young men played the parts of women, since women were considered too delicate. And if it rained while you were performing, the show had to go on. Theaters had walls but not ceilings, so actors and audience alike got wet!

WHEN WAS QUEEN ELIZABETH LIKE A NEWSPAPER—BLACK, WHITE, AND RED ALL OVER?

As the queen grew older, she tried to hide her age. She wore bright *red* wigs and lots of chalky *white* makeup. But she couldn't cover up her *black* teeth. (They had rotted from too many sweets!) Finally the queen ordered every mirror in her palace removed.

Queen Elizabeth loved beautiful clothes and had an enormous, fashionable wardrobe. Her three thousand garments, covered with gems and ermine fur, were a visible sign of her wealth and power. But they must've been awfully uncomfortable! Most garments were too heavy to wash, so they were perfumed instead.

The queen wore so many layers of clothes—eight!—that she needed lots of help getting into or out of her smock, bodice, petticoat, hoops, skirt, kirtle, gown, and sleeves.

Elizabeth's court was unsurpassed in its extravagance and riches. Fashionable men of the time wore padded vests called doublets, silk stockings, and short, puffed breeches stuffed with horsehair. To finish off, a man needed a cloak of the finest velvet or satin, lined with silk and embroidered with gold, silver, or pearls. Courtiers tried to outdo one another, even dying their beards orange or purple to match their coats. It wasn't unusual for people to spend all the money they had on clothes, just to get noticed. The saying was that some wore their fortunes on their backs.

Women wore hooplike skirts called farthingales, which were placed over a thick roll at the waist. Skirts often stretched several feet around and looked like a can—they were the same width all around from hips to feet. High, stiff ruffs made of starched material stuck out in a circle around the neck and were held in place by sticks called stays. Men wore them, too. Ruffs could extend out as much as nine inches! They were draped with jewels to finish them off. Pearls were so rare that only the wealthiest could afford them. But Elizabeth wrapped herself in ropes of them.

TRUE OR FALSE: ENGLAND'S KING JAMES WAS BOTH JAMES I AND JAMES VI.

True. Since Mary Queen of Scots had been beheaded, her son, King James VI of Scotland, was next in line for England's throne. He became King James I of England when Queen Elizabeth died. James had ruled Scotland by *divine right*, which meant he believed that he was chosen by God and could do whatever he wanted. But England was used to having a ruler like Queen Elizabeth, who cared what her people thought and wanted.

I RULE!

Every November 5, the English light bonfires and fireworks to celebrate Guy Fawkes Day and the survival of their government. On November 5, 1605, Guy Fawkes was discovered trying to blow up Parliament. After Fawkes was arrested and wouldn't reveal who had helped him, it was off to the streeeeeetching rack! When the king's men were done with him, Fawkes was so crippled he couldn't even walk to where he was hanged.

TRUE OR FALSE: THE PILGRIMS WERE THE FIRST ENGLISH SETTLEMENT TO SURVIVE IN AMERICA.

False. In 1607—almost twenty years after Sir Walter Raleigh's colony at Roanoke Island mysteriously disappeared, but still thirteen years before the Pilgrims set sail— another group of settlers landed in Virginia. They named their colony James Town (later known as Jamestown), in honor of King James. Times were especially tough for them until they began cultivating a crop called tobacco.

WHY DID ENGLISHMEN GET MAD AT KING CHARLES?

Because he was getting un-*rule*-y! Just like his father, James I, King Charles I was a bossy king. He was so bossy, in fact, that when Parliament wouldn't do what he said, he told all the members of Parliament (or M.P.s) to go home! Then he ruled without them for eleven years. Charles made people pay heavy taxes and told them how to practice their religion. When Parliament was finally allowed to come back, the king got *really* unruly and tried to arrest five M.P.s. Parliament raised an army—it was time for war.

DID THE WAR MEAN KINGS AND QUEENS WERE GONE FOR GOOD?

King Charles was captured in 1646, and no one really knew what to do with him. The Parliament finally got so angry about all the trouble the king had caused that he was executed. The king wore two shirts to his January execution so he wouldn't shiver from the cold and look afraid. Even his enemies said the king faced his death with courage.

Hairstyles told people what side of the war you were on–kind of like a uniform does. People who were on Parliament's side were called Roundheads because their haircuts were short and bowl shaped. People on King Charles's side were called Cavaliers. They wore their hair long like the king's.

OLIVER CROMWELL (1649-1660)

WAS OLIVER CROMWELL A KING?

Since King Charles I was beheaded, you probably guessed that he lost the war. His eldest son and heir, also called Charles, lost his crown to a man named Oliver Cromwell, who'd been one of the leaders against Charles I. Cromwell wasn't a king, even though he acted like he was. He refused the crown and called himself Lord Protector.

DID THE PEOPLE MISS HAVING A KING?

Not at first. But Oliver Cromwell was very strict. He did not allow dancing, theater, music (except hymns), or card playing. So even though Cromwell did some good things like improving education and winning a big victory over Spain, no one really liked him.

Once the monarchy was back in place, Cromwell's dead body was dug up and his head cut off. The head was stuck atop a pole outside the Houses of Parliament to warn people to obey the king. We think the head stayed there for a whopping twenty years, until it was blown down by a heavy wind.

WOULD IT BE SO BAD TO HAVE A KING AGAIN?

This is the question Englishmen started asking themselves. When Oliver Cromwell died, his son Richard took his place and was a poor ruler. So the people invited Charles II, King Charles I's son, to claim the throne that had really been his all along.

WHAT WAS KING CHARLES II'S LEAST FAVORITE GAME?

Probably hide-and-seek. When his father, King Charles I, was beheaded, King Charles II decided he'd be safer living in France than keeping the crown. To get to France, he had to disguise himself and travel through enemy territory in England and Wales.

DID KING CHARLES II PLAY BY THE RULES?

He had to, to get the crown back. The English people didn't want another bossy king, so Parliament made Charles II promise two things: He would rule *with* Parliament, and he would be Protestant, not Catholic. Charles didn't want to do either of these things, but he agreed so he could be king.

WAS KING CHARLES A VOLUNTEER FIREFIGHTER?

He was, during the Great Fire of London in 1666. The fire started in a baker's oven, and wind spread the flames to all the city's wooden houses. The fire raged for three days and destroyed most of London. People fought it with leather

buckets of water from the River Thames. The king himself helped fight the fire until his clothes and face were black.

The crown jewels are kept at the Tower of London. The Royal Scepter, a long wand held in the monarch's right hand during coronation, contains the Star of Africa, one of the world's biggest diamonds. The royal crown is made of solid gold and 440 glittering gems.

MARY II (1689-1694)
& WILLIAM III (1689-1702)

WHY DID KING WILLIAM III AND QUEEN MARY II RULE ENGLAND TOGETHER?

William and Mary were a package deal. They were married to each other, and both were heirs to the throne. Mary was the daughter of King James II, who ruled after Charles II, and William was James's nephew. Since James was stubborn, straitlaced, and Catholic, he wasn't very popular. So the Protestant William and Mary were invited to come and rule instead. They agreed, and James ran away to France.

Queen Mary came to love her husband dearly, but she didn't when their marriage was first arranged. She cried through their entire wedding ceremony!

WHAT WERE WILLIAM AND MARY GOOD AT SHARING?

Power. William and Mary began to share power with Parliament when they agreed to the "Glorious Revolution"

in 1688. In the Revolution, which got its name because it happened peacefully, Parliament and the monarchy agreed to become more equal partners. Since then, Parliament has had the final say in making laws, and in approving the next King or Queen. William and Mary agreed to these changes to help make England healthy and strong.

ANNE (1702-1714)

WHAT WAS SO GOOD ABOUT "GOOD QUEEN ANNE"?

Queen Anne was likable, loyal, and proud of England. Her stable reign was good for her country. Anne helped England become rich and powerful by declaring war on France and winning land and trading rights in North America.

A lady-in-waiting is a queen's personal servant and companion. Queen Anne's lady-in-waiting was her best friend and childhood playmate, Sarah Jennings. Sarah gave Anne lots of advice. She also oversaw the ladies who dressed the queen and made sure the clothes in the royal wardrobe were neat and tidy.

WHEN DID GREAT BRITAIN BECOME GREAT?

During Queen Anne's reign, England and Scotland officially became united. The Act of Union in 1707 created Great Britain, which is made up of the countries of England, Wales, and Scotland. The countries have separate schools, legal courts, and churches, but the same flag, coins, Parliament, and king or queen. So now the English monarch was the British monarch.

WHY DIDN'T KING GEORGE III'S GREAT-GRANDFATHER, KING GEORGE I, SPEAK ENGLISH?

Because he was German! Parliament had decided in 1701 that all England's kings and queens had to be Protestant, and George I was the closest relative.

DOES GREAT BRITAIN HAVE A PRESIDENT?

Well, kind of. Only he or she is called the prime minister. This job started when King George I was in power, as he didn't really want to rule England. George spent as much time as he could back in Germany and left most of his decisions to a prime minister.

DID FARMER GEORGE MILK COWS AND PLOW FIELDS?

No. But King George III got that nickname because he loved to be out in the country, visiting with his people. He was so fascinated with farming that he created his own farm at Windsor Castle. Unlike Kings George I and George II before him, King George III was born and raised in England—and proud of it. He never once left the country.

King George III was once found talking to an oak tree. Poor George! For the last ten years of his reign, he was blind and not quite right in the head.

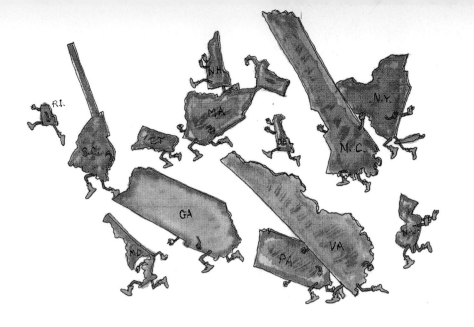

WHAT THIRTEEN BRITISH COLONIES WON THEIR FREEDOM DURING KING GEORGE III'S REIGN?

Hint: One of the colonies was named for Queen Elizabeth I, the Virgin Queen.

That's right, the American colonies! The colonies fought a war against King George III because they wanted a say in their own government. They didn't like being ruled by a king who was all the way across the ocean. The colonies won the war in 1783.

WHAT DOES A KING DO WHEN HE BUYS A NEW HOUSE?

He doubles the number of rooms and calls it a palace! Buckingham Palace, the monarch's main London home since 1837, has 602 rooms. (Aren't you glad you're not the maid?) Queen Elizabeth II lives in the palace today. When the queen is in, the British flag flies above the house.

A building called 10 Downing Street has been the prime minister's home since 1732. Unlike the enormous White House, where the U.S. president lives, the prime minister's house is just a regular little row house on a quiet street.

VICTORIA (1837-1901)

WHICH BRITISH MONARCH HOLDS THE RECORD FOR LIVING AND RULING THE LONGEST?

Queen Victoria. She ruled for sixty-three years and lived to be eighty-two years old. George III comes in second. He ruled for fifty-nine years and lived to be eighty-one. Queen Victoria reigned for so long and during such changing times that the whole period became known as the Victorian Age.

TRUE OR FALSE: QUEEN VICTORIA WAS ALSO EMPRESS OF INDIA.

True. In fact, Queen Victoria ruled over not only Great Britain and India, but also one quarter of the world's land and people! During Victoria's reign, Britain's great navy won colonies around the globe. It was said that "the sun never set on the British empire." Now you know part of the reason English is spoken in so many countries around the world!

Victoria was only eighteen years old when she became queen. Even though she'd had a good education, she had a lot to learn about ruling. So her prime minister, Lord Melbourne, became her trusted friend and advisor.

WAS QUEEN VICTORIA'S FAVORITE COLOR BLACK?

No. But Queen Victoria wore black for the last forty years of her life. She did this to show she was in mourning for Prince Albert, her beloved husband, who died when he was only forty-two. Victoria had loved him so much that, for thirteen years after his death, she stayed in her palace and didn't appear at a single public function.

LONGEST REIGN

IF YOU WERE A NINE- OR TEN-YEAR-OLD FROM A POOR VICTORIAN FAMILY, WHERE MIGHT YOU SPEND TWELVE HOURS EACH DAY?

A. playing kickball in the street with your buddies

B. watching cartoons on TV

C. working in a coal mine or factory

D. sitting in school learning how to read and write

Unfortunately, the answer is *c*. During Queen Victoria's reign, new inventions spurred the *Industrial Revolution*, which changed the way people lived and worked. Jobs that had once been done by hand at home (like sewing) could now be done much faster in big, noisy, dirty factories. Children got the worst jobs—like crawling inside dangerous machines to fix them. School doesn't sound so bad after all, does it?! Good thing Queen Victoria helped pass laws that made working days shorter and safer.

Cities, factories, and even royal palaces were dirty places in these days. Queen Victoria hired men to be royal rat catchers and bug destroyers!

39

Why might it be difficult for two Victorian women to sit on the same couch? Because their skirts were so big! It was high fashion in Queen Victoria's day for ladies to wear, under their dresses, round metal "cages" that made their skirts stick out many feet around them.

WHERE IN ENGLAND COULD YOU GO TO SEE THE LATEST INVENTIONS?

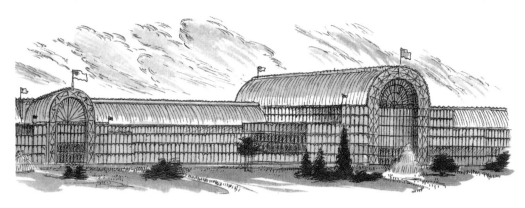

The Great Exhibition of 1851, which was held in an enormous glass structure called the Crystal Palace. The Exhibition, organized by Prince Albert, was a showcase of one hundred thousand objects and new inventions from England and around the world. Millions of people came to see everything from machines and railway engines to fancy furniture and jewelry.

WHAT'S "BEN" RINGING AT THE HOUSES OF PARLIAMENT SINCE 1858?

Many people think it's a clock tower called Big Ben. But Big Ben isn't the tower; it's actually the huge bell that rings inside it.

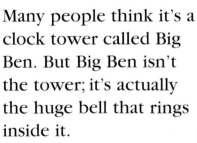

WHY DID GEORGE V CHANGE HIS LAST NAME?

To make it a bit more friendly. "Saxe-Coburg and Gotha" is certainly a mouthful! Even worse was that the name was German—and England was at war with Germany. Some people thought the king might be secretly on Germany's side because part of his family was German.

To prove those people wrong, King George V adopted a very English name. He chose Windsor, after the town where one of England's oldest royal palaces is. Windsor Castle is the royal family's main home outside of London.

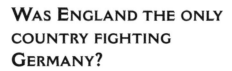

King George V was the first British monarch to speak to his subjects on the radio. People felt closer to their king since they could hear his voice instead of just reading about him in the newspaper. In 1932 King George V started a tradition of addressing the nation every Christmas.

WAS ENGLAND THE ONLY COUNTRY FIGHTING GERMANY?

No. England was fighting in World War I, and it wasn't called a world war for nothing. Most of the world's powerful nations, including the United States, were fighting against Germany and its friends to keep them from taking over land that wasn't theirs. By the end of the awful four-year war, as many as thirteen million people, nearly one million of them British, had died.

King George VI was the first member of the royal family to fly a plane, which he did in the royal navy.

WHY WAS GEORGE VI SURPRISED TO BECOME KING?

King George VI was the second, not the oldest, son of King George V. George V's oldest son, Edward VIII, had become king when his father died, but he was king for less than a year. Edward *abdicated,* or gave up, the throne because he wanted to marry a divorced American woman, which the Church of England wouldn't allow if he were king.

WHY DID KING GEORGE'S WIFE SAY, "I'M GLAD WE'VE BEEN BOMBED"?

No, she wasn't crazy! During World War II, German planes dropped bombs all over London. When the royal family's home at Buckingham Palace was bombed, the queen was able to understand how her fellow Londoners felt. Buckingham Palace was bombed nine times—once about one hundred feet from where the king was sitting.

"Never give in, never give in, never, never, never, never—in nothing great or small, large or petty—never give in except to convictions of honor and good sense."

—Prime Minister Winston Churchill

WHO WAS ENGLAND'S PRIME MINISTER DURING WORLD WAR II?

Winston Churchill. He was famous for his inspiring speeches and determination to beat Germany. He was also known for the V for Victory signs he made with his pointer and middle fingers. Try it!

ELIZABETH II (1952-)

IS QUEEN ELIZABETH II ENGLAND'S FIRST ROYAL TV STAR?

Queen Elizabeth II might not be a glamorous actress or talk show host, but she was the first monarch whose coronation was shown on TV. Twenty million people watched the ceremony.

TRUE OR FALSE: QUEEN ELIZABETH II MAKES BRITAIN'S LAWS.

False. Today it's not the queen who's in charge, but the prime minister. The prime minister and Parliament make laws together, kind of like the way America's president and Congress do. The queen can give her opinion, but it might not be followed.

A few British people think it's silly to have kings and queens because they're not really needed anymore. But most people can't imagine getting rid of all the tradition and history of the royal family. Can you believe that Queen Elizabeth II is a direct descendant of William the Conqueror? Wow!

SO WHAT *IS* THE QUEEN'S JOB?

The queen's most important job is to represent her country, at home and around the world. She's a special symbol of Great Britain. The queen and her family spend lots of time working with groups that help the poor and others.

DOES THE QUEEN EARN A LARGE SALARY?

With all those palaces and crown jewels, she must, right? Actually, Parliament gives the queen money to use for royal business, but the queen doesn't get a paycheck for being queen.

THE MONARCHY TODAY AND IN THE FUTURE

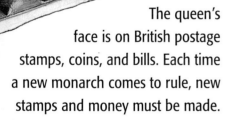

DOES ENGLAND STILL RULE MORE THAN ONE QUARTER OF THE WORLD'S LAND AND PEOPLE?

Not anymore. Many of the countries Queen Victoria ruled over are now independent. But more than fifty of those countries are still part of a kind of family of nations called the British Commonwealth. The countries of the Commonwealth work together to reach common goals. The queen is the head of the Commonwealth.

IS THERE A PRINCE OF ENGLAND?

Well, sort of. Except he's called the Prince of Wales. (Not the kind of whales that live in the ocean—England's neighbor country, Wales!) King Edward I took over Wales in 1284. He later gave his oldest son, who was next in line for the throne, the title of Prince of Wales. The Prince of Wales was once involved in the government of Wales, but today his main job is getting ready to be king.

The queen's face is on British postage stamps, coins, and bills. Each time a new monarch comes to rule, new stamps and money must be made.

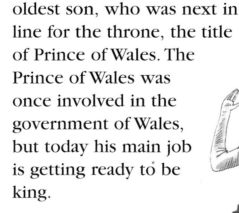

WHAT'S IT LIKE TO BE A ROYAL KID TODAY?

WHO MIGHT BE THE NEXT KING OR QUEEN OF ENGLAND?

Could you get the job? Sorry, but the heir to the throne is still the ruling monarch's oldest son. The next person in line for the throne is Prince Charles, Queen Elizabeth's oldest son. If anything happened to him, the crown would go to his oldest son, Prince William.

WHERE DO ROYAL KIDS GO TO SCHOOL?

Queen Elizabeth II and the kings and queens before her were taught at home by tutors. But Queen Elizabeth thought it would be good for her kids to go to school like other children. Prince Charles and his late wife, Diana, also sent their sons, William and Harry, to school.

Prince Charles might've wished he'd had a tutor. At school he was always teased about his big ears. Reporters bothered his classmates for gossip about him. Someone even stole his English notebook, and his essays were printed in magazines. Being a prince isn't always so charming!

Is being a royal kid today great or a royal pain in the neck? You decide:

ROYAL TREATMENT	ROYAL PAIN IN THE NECK

People would call you "your royal highness" and bow. Your nanny would feed and clothe you, take you to the park, and make sure you were clean and well mannered.

Your parents, the king and queen, would be away a lot, so you'd probably see your nanny more than your mom and dad.

With your nanny, you could wear casual clothes like jeans and T-shirts. You could play sports, go to movies, and eat burgers and fries like a normal kid.

You'd live in your own apartment in Buckingham Palace, next door to your parents.

Reporters and TV cameras would follow you every time you left the palace. Maybe it would be better to stay home and have dinner with the king and queen, even though you'd have to dress formally, bow, and call them "your royal highness." You could only speak to them when spoken to.

Sometimes you might live at Windsor Castle or other royal palaces. You'd travel for official public events.

When you went off to school to be with other kids, your bodyguards would keep you from getting kidnapped. You might also wear an electronic tracking bracelet, like Prince William does, that would keep you in constant touch with palace security. You'd have a private car and chauffeur and maybe even a footman to wait on you.

To get to the events, you'd have to fly on a separate airplane from the king and queen, in case of an accident. Once you arrived, you'd have to sit through lots of fancy ceremonies.

The bodyguards would be with you every second of the day. Imagine how hard it would be to go out with friends, or on a date!

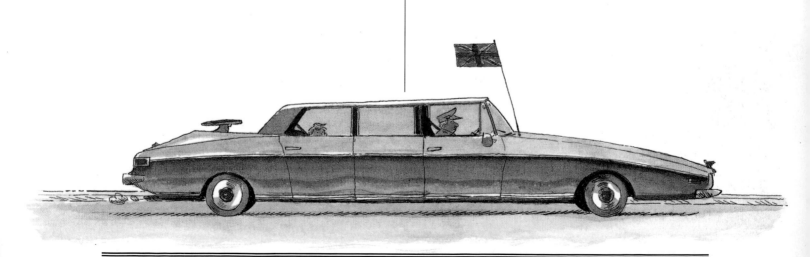

THE KINGS AND QUEENS OF ENGLAND (AND LATER THE UNITED KINGDOM)

SAXONS AND DANES	REIGN
Egbert, King of Wessex	802–839
Ethelwulf	839–855
Ethelbald	855–860
Ethelbert	860–866
Ethelred	866–871
Alfred the Great	871–899
Edward the Elder	899–924
Athelstan	924–939
Edmund I	939–946
Edred	946–955
Edwy	955–959
Edgar	959–975
Edward II the Martyr	975–979
Ethelred II the Unready	979–1013
	and 1014–1016
Sweyn	1013–1014
Edmund II Ironside	Apr.–Nov. 1016
Canute the Great	1016–1035
Harold Harefoot	1035–1037
(jointly with) Hardicanute	
Harold Harefoot (alone)	1037–1040
Hardicanute (alone)	1040–1042
Edward III the Confessor	1042–1066
Harold II	Jan.–Oct. 1066
Edgar Atheling	Oct.–Dec. 1066

HOUSE OF NORMANDY	
William I the Conqueror	1066–1087
William II Rufus	1087–1100
Henry I Beauclerc	1100–1135
Stephen	1135–1154

HOUSE OF ANGEVIN	
Henry II Curtmantle	1154–1189
Richard I Lionheart	1189–1199
John Lackland	1199–1216

HOUSE OF PLANTAGENET	
Henry III	1216–1272
Edward I Longshanks	1272–1307
Edward II	1307–1327
Edward III	1327–1377
Richard II	1377–1399

HOUSE OF LANCASTER	
Henry IV	1399–1413
Henry V	1413–1422
Henry VI	1422–1461
	and 1470–1471

HOUSE OF YORK	REIGN
Edward IV	1461–1470
	and 1471–1483
Edward V	Apr.–June 1483
Richard III	1483–1485

HOUSE OF TUDOR	
Henry VII	1485–1509
Henry VIII	1509–1547
Edward VI	1547–1553
Jane	July 10–19, 1553
Mary I	1553–1558
Elizabeth I	1558–1603

HOUSE OF STUART	
James I	1603–1625
Charles I	1625–1649
Commonwealth	1649–1660
Charles II	1660–1685
James II	1685–1688
Mary II and William III	1689–1694
William III (alone)	1694–1702
Anne	1702–1714

HOUSE OF HANOVER	
George I	1714–1727
George II	1727–1760
George III	1760–1820
George IV	1820–1830
William IV	1830–1837
Victoria	1837–1901

HOUSE OF SAXE-COBURG AND GOTHA	
Edward VII	1901–1910

HOUSE OF WINDSOR	
George V	1910–1936
Edward VIII	Jan.–Dec. 1936
George VI	1936–1952
Elizabeth II	1952–